THE *New* Easter Triduum

The New Easter Triduum
Published by **Redemptorist Publications**
Alphonsus House, Chawton, Hampshire, GU34 3HQ
Email rp@rpbooks.co.uk, www.rpbooks.co.uk
A registered charity limited by guarantee.
Registered in England 3261721

This compilation © Redemptorist Publications, 2012

First published 1994
This revised edition first published February 2012
Tenth printing February 2012

General Editor: Denis McBride C.Ss.R.
Editors: Peter Edwards and Andrew Lyon
Design: Eliana Thompson

ISBN 978-0-85231-391-6

Acknowledgements: Excerpts from the English translation of
The Roman Missal © 2010, International Commission on English
in the Liturgy Corporation. The Grail Psalter (by permission of
The Grail, England and HarperCollins & Co. Ltd); Bible readings
are taken from the JERUSALEM BIBLE © 1966, 1967, 1968 by
Darton, Longman & Todd Ltd, and Doubleday and Company Inc.
and are used by permission of the Publishers. All rights reserved.

Concordat cum originali Ann Blackett
Imprimatur + Kieran Conry, Bishop of Arundel and Brighton,
7 February 2012.
Permission granted for distribution in dioceses of Scotland

Printed by Joseph Ball (Printers) Ltd
Leicester LE2 5LQ

The Easter Triduum

An introduction

During the Sacred Triduum (the word comes from the Latin, meaning "three days"), we come together to celebrate the heart of our faith – the passion, death and resurrection of our Lord Jesus Christ.

Jesus Christ came to show us the meaning and purpose of life. In his own life on earth he revealed to us what it is to be fully human as God created us to be. He showed us how to live, how to relate to one another, how to build a relationship with our heavenly Father.

In his passion, death and resurrection, he confirmed that what he had revealed and promised was true:

- This is God's world and God has power over all life and death.
- Nothing that can happen to us in life or death can separate us from God's love for us.
- In death, life is changed, not ended.

We have spent the past six weeks preparing to celebrate this feast of feasts. We have reflected on our personal failure to follow Christ in our thoughts, words and deeds. We have tried to make amends for the harm we have done by our actions or by our inaction. Try to make time, if you have not done so already, to receive the sacrament of reconciliation and so truly enter into the spirit of new life when you renew your baptismal vows at the Easter Vigil.

Lord Jesus Christ, you are the Lamb of God, you take away the sins of the world. Through the grace of the Holy Spirit restore me to friendship with your Father, cleanse me from every stain of sin in the blood you shed for me, and raise me to new life for the glory of your name. Amen.

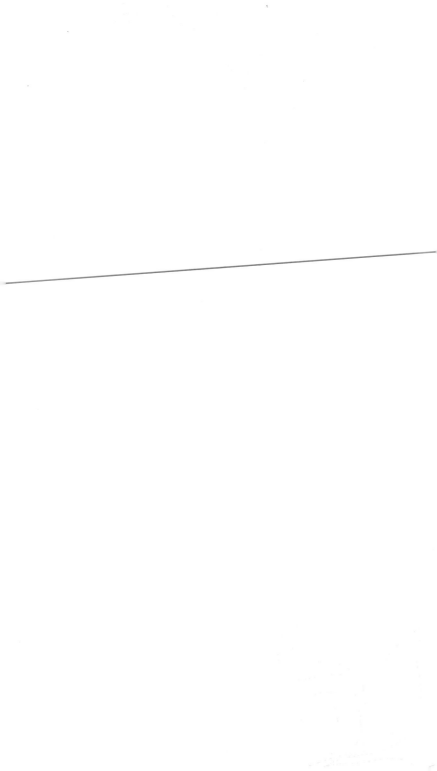

Contents

Maundy Thursday

This morning in cathedrals around the world, priests and people gathered with their bishop for the Chrism Mass. The oils that will be used in our parishes and in our communities throughout the coming year are prepared and blessed before they are first used in our Easter Vigil. The Oil of Baptism and the Oil of the Sick are solemnly blessed, the Oil of Chrism is blessed and consecrated.

This evening, we come together as a community of believers to celebrate the feast day of the Eucharist. On this night we call to mind what Jesus said and did at the Last Supper. We are reminded that he washed the feet of his disciples and so gave us a clear example of the way in which we are to follow him: in loving service to others. Jesus then gave himself to his disciples in his gift of the Eucharist, calling them to share in his mission: to do what he had done.

Evening Mass of the Lord's Supper

Entrance Antiphon

We should glory in the Cross of our Lord Jesus Christ, in whom is our salvation, life and resurrection, through whom we are saved and delivered.

The Gloria is said or sung. While it is being sung, the church bells are rung, and then they remain silent until the Gloria of the Easter Vigil.

Collect

O God, who have called us to participate
in this most sacred Supper,
in which your Only Begotten Son,
when about to hand himself over to death,
entrusted to the Church a sacrifice new for all eternity,
the banquet of his love,
grant, we pray,
that we may draw from so great a mystery,
the fullness of charity and of life.
Through our Lord Jesus Christ, your Son,
who lives and reigns with you in the unity of the Holy Spirit,
one God, for ever and ever.
Amen.

First Reading (Exodus 12:1-8. 11-14)

A reading from the book of Exodus

The Lord said to Moses and Aaron in the land of Egypt, "This month is to be the first of all the others for you, the first month of your year. Speak to the whole community of Israel and say, 'On the tenth day of this month each man must take an animal from the flock, one for each family: one animal for each household. If the household is too small to eat the animal, a man must join with his neighbour, the nearest to his house, as the number of persons requires. You must take into account what each can eat in deciding the number for the animal. It must be an animal without blemish, a male one year old; you may take it from either sheep or goats. You must keep it till the fourteenth day of the month when the whole assembly of the community of Israel shall slaughter it between the two evenings. Some of the blood must then be taken and put on the two doorposts and the lintel of the houses where it is eaten. That night, the flesh is to be eaten, roasted over the fire; it must be eaten with unleavened bread and bitter herbs. You shall eat it like this: with a girdle round your waist, sandals on your feet, a staff in your hand. You shall eat it hastily: it is a passover in honour of the Lord. That night, I will go through the land of Egypt and strike down all the first-born in the land of Egypt, man and beast alike, and I shall deal out punishment to all the gods of Egypt, I am the Lord. The blood shall serve to mark the houses that you live in. When I see the blood I will pass over you and you shall escape the destroying plague when I strike the land of Egypt. This day is to be a day of remembrance for you, and you must celebrate it as a feast in the Lord's honour. For all generations you are to declare it a day of festival, for ever.'"

The word of the Lord.

Psalm (Psalm 115)

Response: **The blessing-cup that we bless is a communion with the blood of Christ.**

1   How can I repay the Lord
     for his goodness to me?
     The cup of salvation I will raise;
     I will call on the Lord's name. R.

2   O precious in the eyes of the Lord
     is the death of his faithful.
     Your servant, Lord, your servant am I;
     you have loosened my bonds. R.

3   A thanksgiving sacrifice I make:
     I will call on the Lord's name.
     My vows to the Lord I will fulfil
     before all his people. R.

Second Reading (1 Corinthians 11:23-26)

A reading from the first letter of St Paul to the Corinthians

This is what I received from the Lord, and in turn passed on to you: that on the same night that he was betrayed, the Lord Jesus took some bread, and thanked God for it and broke it, and he said, "This is my body, which is for you; do this as a memorial of me." In the same way he took the cup after supper, and said, "This cup is the new covenant in my blood. Whenever you drink it, do this as a memorial of me." Until the Lord comes, therefore, every time you eat this bread and drink this cup, you are proclaiming his death.

The word of the Lord.

Gospel Acclamation

Praise and honour to you, Lord Jesus!
I give you a new commandment:
love one another just as I have loved you,
**   says the Lord.**
Praise and honour to you, Lord Jesus!

Gospel (John 13:1-15)

A reading from the holy Gospel according to John

It was before the festival of the Passover, and Jesus knew that the hour had come for him to pass from this world to the Father. He had always loved those who were his in the world, but now he showed how perfect his love was.

They were at supper, and the devil had already put it into the mind of Judas Iscariot son of Simon, to betray him. Jesus knew that the Father had put everything into his hands, and that he had come from God and was returning to God, and he got up from table, removed his outer garment and, taking a towel, wrapped it round his waist; he then poured water into a basin and began to wash the disciples' feet and to wipe them with the towel he was wearing.

He came to Simon Peter, who said to him, "Lord, are you going to wash my feet?" Jesus answered, "At the moment you do not know what I am doing, but later you will understand." "Never!" said Peter "You shall never wash my feet." Jesus replied, "If I do not wash you, you can have nothing in common with me." "Then, Lord," said Simon Peter, "not only my feet, but my hands and my head as well!" Jesus said, "No one who has taken a bath needs washing, he is clean all over. You too are clean, though not all of you are." He knew who was going to betray him, that was why he said, "though not all of you are".

When he had washed their feet and put on his clothes again he went back to the table. "Do you understand", he said, "what I have done to you? You call me Master and Lord, and rightly; so I am. If I, then, the Lord and Master, have washed your feet, you should wash each other's feet. I have given you an example so that you may copy what I have done to you."

The Gospel of the Lord.

Washing of Feet

Some of the following antiphons or other suitable songs may be sung.

Antiphon 1

After the Lord had risen from supper,
he poured water into a basin
and began to wash the feet of his disciples:
he left them this example.

Antiphon 2

The Lord Jesus, after eating supper with his disciples,
washed their feet and said to them:
Do you know what I, your Lord and Master, have done for you?
I have given you an example, that you should do likewise.

Antiphon 3

Lord, are you to wash my feet? Jesus said to him in answer:
If I do not wash your feet, you will have no share with me.
V. So he came to Simon Peter and Peter said to him:
Lord, are you to wash my feet...
V. What I am doing, you do not know for now,
but later you will come to know.
Lord, are you to wash my feet...

Antiphon 4

If I, your Lord and Master, have washed your feet,
how much more should you wash each other's feet?

Antiphon 5

This is how all will know that you are my disciples:
if you have love for one another.
V. Jesus said to his disciples:
This is how all will know that you are my disciples:
if you have love for one another.

Antiphon 6

I give you a new commandment,
that you love one another
as I have loved you, says the Lord.

Antiphon 7

Let faith, hope and charity, these three, remain among you,
but the greatest of these is charity.
V. Now faith, hope and charity, these three, remain;
but the greatest of these is charity.
Let faith, hope and charity, these three, remain among you,
but the greatest of these is charity.

Procession of the Gifts

Gifts for those who are poor may be brought to
the altar, together with the bread and wine. The
following or another suitable song may be sung.

Antiphon

Where true charity is dwelling, God is present there.

V. By the love of Christ we have been brought together:
V. let us find in him our gladness and our pleasure;
V. may we love him and revere him, God the living,
V. and in love respect each other with sincere hearts.

Where true charity is dwelling, God is present there.

V. So when we as one are gathered all together,
V. let us strive to keep our minds free of division;
V. may there be an end to malice, strife and quarrels;
V. and let Christ our God be dwelling here among us.

Where true charity is dwelling, God is present there.

V. May your face thus be our vision, bright in glory,
V. Christ our God, with all the blessed Saints in heaven:
V. such delight is pure and faultless, joy unbounded,
V. which endures through countless ages world without end.
   Amen.

Prayer over the Offerings

Grant us, O Lord, we pray,
that we may participate worthily in these mysteries,
for whenever the memorial of this sacrifice is celebrated
the work of our redemption is accomplished.
Through Christ our Lord.
Amen.

The Eucharistic Prayer

The Lord be with you.
And with your spirit.

Lift up your hearts.
We lift them up to the Lord.

Let us give thanks to the Lord our God.
It is right and just.

It is truly right and just, our duty and our salvation,
always and everywhere to give you thanks,
Lord, holy Father, almighty and eternal God,
through Christ our Lord.

For he is the true and eternal Priest,
who instituted the pattern of an everlasting sacrifice
and was the first to offer himself as the saving Victim,
commanding us to make this offering as his memorial.
As we eat his flesh that was sacrificed for us,
we are made strong,
and, as we drink his Blood that was poured out for us,
we are washed clean.
And so, with Angels and Archangels,

with Thrones and Dominions,
and with all the hosts and Powers of heaven,
we sing the hymn of your glory,
as without end we acclaim:

Holy, Holy, Holy Lord God of hosts.
Heaven and earth are full of your glory.
Hosanna in the highest.
Blessed is he who comes in the name of the Lord.
Hosanna in the highest.

Communion Antiphon

This is the Body that will be given up for you;
this is the Chalice of the new covenant in my Blood,
**   says the Lord;**
do this, whenever you receive it, in memory of me.

Prayer after Communion

Grant, almighty God,
that, just as we are renewed
by the Supper of your Son in this present age,
so we may enjoy his banquet for all eternity.
Who lives and reigns for ever and ever.
Amen.

Transfer of the Most Blessed Sacrament

The following or another Eucharistic song may
be sung.

1   Of the glorious Body telling,
        O my tongue, its mysteries sing,
        And the Blood, all price excelling,
        Which the world's eternal King,
        In a noble womb once dwelling,
        Shed for the world's ransoming.

2   Given for us, for us descending,
     Of a Virgin to proceed,
     Man with man in converse blending,
     Scattered he the Gospel seed,
     Till his sojourn drew to ending,
     Which he closed in wondrous deed.

3   At the last great Supper lying
     Circled by his brethren's band,
     Meekly with the law complying,
     First he finished its command,
     Then, immortal Food supplying,
     Gave himself with his own hand.

4   Word made Flesh, by word he maketh
     Very bread his Flesh to be;
     Man in wine Christ's Blood partaketh:
     And if senses fail to see,
     Faith alone the true heart waketh
     To behold the mystery.

As the priest incenses the Blessed Sacrament in the
tabernacle at the place of repose, the following two
verses or another Eucharistic song may be sung.

5   Therefore we, before him bending,
     This great Sacrament revere;
     Types and shadows have their ending,
     For the newer rite is here;
     Faith, our outward sense befriending,
     Makes the inward vision clear.

6   Glory let us give, and blessing
     To the Father and the Son;
     Honour, might, and praise addressing,
     While eternal ages run;
     Ever too his love confessing,
     Who, from both, with both is one.
     Amen.

Good Friday

The word "Good" in the name we give to this day originates from an old sense of the word, meaning "holy". Today we commemorate the sufferings and death of Jesus Christ. Our liturgy will take us through three stages as we unite ourselves with him in his suffering and sacrifice for love of all people.

- We listen to the word of God. In the prophecy of Isaiah, in the letter to the Hebrews and, most importantly of all, in St John's account of our Lord's Passion, we discover the depth of love shown in Christ's sufferings. We respond to his love in praying for the welfare of the whole world, that Christ's love may reach the hearts of all men and women.
- The cross on which Christ suffered and died is the sign of God's love that won life for the world and so each one of us is now personally invited to venerate the cross.
- Finally, we receive Holy Communion. Jesus Christ died to make us one in love and truth. He called us to be reconciled with him and with one another. In Holy Communion we are made one.

As we leave the church in silence we contemplate the gift of Christ's suffering.

The Celebration of the Passion of the Lord

The priest and ministers go to the altar in silence.
All kneel as the priest and deacon prostrate themselves,
then stand as the priest goes to the chair.

Prayer

Remember your mercies, O Lord,
and with your eternal protection sanctify your servants,
for whom Christ your Son,
by the shedding of his Blood,
established the Paschal Mystery.
Who lives and reigns for ever and ever.
Amen.

or

O God, who by the Passion of Christ your Son, our Lord,
abolished the death inherited from ancient sin
by every succeeding generation,
grant that just as, being conformed to him,
we have borne by the law of nature
the image of the man of earth,
so by the sanctification of grace
we may bear the image of the Man of heaven.
Through Christ our Lord.
Amen.

First Part
THE LITURGY OF THE WORD

First Reading (Isaiah 52:13 – 53:12)
A reading from the prophet Isaiah

See, my servant will prosper,
he shall be lifted up, exalted, rise to great heights.

As the crowds were appalled on seeing him
– so disfigured did he look
that he seemed no longer human –
so will the crowds be astonished at him,
and kings stand speechless before him;
for they shall see something never told
and witness something never heard before:
"Who could believe what we have heard,
and to whom has the power of the Lord been revealed?"

Like a sapling he grew up in front of us,
like a root in arid ground.
Without beauty, without majesty (we saw him),
no looks to attract our eyes;
a thing despised and rejected by men,
a man of sorrows and familiar with suffering,
a man to make people screen their faces;
he was despised and we took no account of him.

And yet ours were the sufferings he bore,
ours the sorrows he carried.
But we, we thought of him as someone punished,
struck by God, and brought low.
Yet he was pierced through for our faults,
crushed for our sins.
On him lies a punishment that brings us peace,
and through his wounds we are healed.

We had all gone astray like sheep,
each taking his own way,
and the Lord burdened him
with the sins of all of us.
Harshly dealt with, he bore it humbly,
he never opened his mouth,
like a lamb that is led to the slaughter-house,
like a sheep that is dumb before its shearers
never opening its mouth.

By force and by law he was taken;
would anyone plead his cause?
Yes, he was torn away from the land of the living;
for our faults struck down in death.
They gave him a grave with the wicked,
a tomb with the rich,
though he had done no wrong
and there had been no perjury in his mouth.
The Lord has been pleased to crush him with suffering.
If he offers his life in atonement,
he shall see his heirs, he shall have a long life
and through him what the Lord wishes will be done.

His soul's anguish over
he shall see the light and be content.
By his sufferings shall my servant justify many,
taking their faults on himself.

Hence I will grant whole hordes for his tribute,
he shall divide the spoil with the mighty,
for surrendering himself to death
and letting himself be taken for a sinner,
while he was bearing the faults of many
and praying all the time for sinners.
    The word of the Lord.

Psalm (Psalm 30)

Response: Father, into your hands I commend my spirit.

1   In you, O Lord, I take refuge.
    Let me never be put to shame.
    In your justice, set me free.
    Into your hands I commend my spirit.
    It is you who will redeem me, Lord. R.

2   In the face of all my foes
    I am a reproach,
        an object of scorn to my neighbours
        and of fear to my friends. R.

3   Those who see me in the street
    run far away from me.
    I am like a dead man, forgotten in men's hearts,
    like a thing thrown away. R.

4   But as for me, I trust in you, Lord,
    I say: "You are my God."
    My life is in your hands, deliver me
    from the hands of those who hate me. R.

5   Let your face shine on your servant.
    Save me in your love.
    Be strong, let your heart take courage,
    all who hope in the Lord. R.

Second Reading (Hebrews 4:14-16; 5:7-9)
A reading from the letter to the Hebrews

Since in Jesus, the Son of God, we have the supreme high priest who has gone through to the highest heaven, we must never let go of the faith that we have professed. For it is not as if we had a high priest who was incapable of feeling our weaknesses with us; but we have one who has been tempted in every way that we are, though he is without sin. Let us be confident, then, in approaching the throne of grace, that we shall have mercy from him and find grace when we are in need of help.

During his life on earth, he offered up prayer and entreaty, aloud and in silent tears, to the one who had the power to save him out of death, and he submitted so humbly that his prayer was heard. Although he was Son, he learnt to obey through suffering; but having been made perfect, he became for all who obey him the source of eternal salvation.

The word of the Lord.

Gospel Acclamation

Glory and praise to you, O Christ!
Christ was humbler yet,
even to accepting death, death on a cross.
But God raised him high
and gave him the name which is above all names.
Glory and praise to you, O Christ!

Symbols for narration of the Passion:

† for the words of Christ;   N for the narrator;

S for individual voices;   C for the crowd.

Gospel (John 18:1 – 19:42)
The passion of our Lord Jesus Christ according to John

N   Jesus left with his disciples and crossed the Kedron valley. There was a garden there, and he went into it with his disciples. Judas the traitor knew the place well, since Jesus had often met his disciples there, and he brought the cohort to this place together with a detachment of guards sent by the chief priests and the Pharisees, all with lanterns and torches and weapons. Knowing everything that was going to happen to him, Jesus then came forward and said,

†   Who are you looking for?

N They answered,

C Jesus the Nazarene.

N He said,

✝ I am he.

N Now Judas the traitor was standing among them. When Jesus said, "I am he", they moved back and fell to the ground. He asked them a second time,

✝ Who are you looking for?

N They said,

C Jesus the Nazarene.

N Jesus replied,

✝ I have told you that I am he. If I am the one you are looking for, let these others go.

N This was to fulfil the words he had spoken, "Not one of those you gave me have I lost." Simon Peter, who carried a sword, drew it and wounded the high priest's servant, cutting off his right ear. The servant's name was Malchus. Jesus said to Peter,

✝ Put your sword back in its scabbard; am I not to drink the cup that the Father has given me?

N The cohort and its captain and the Jewish guards seized Jesus and bound him. They took him first to Annas, because Annas was the father-in-law of Caiaphas, who was high priest that year. It was Caiaphas who had suggested to the Jews, "It is better for one man to die for the people."
Simon Peter, with another disciple, followed Jesus. This disciple, who was known to the high priest, went with Jesus into the high priest's palace, but Peter stayed outside the door. So the other disciple, the one known to the high priest, went out, spoke to the woman who was keeping the door and brought Peter in. The maid on duty at the door said to Peter,

S Aren't you another of that man's disciples?

N He answered,

S I am not.

N Now it was cold, and the servants and guards had lit a charcoal fire and were standing there warming themselves; so Peter stood there too, warming himself with the others.

The high priest questioned Jesus about his disciples and his teaching. Jesus answered,

✝ I have spoken openly for all the world to hear; I have always taught in the synagogue and in the Temple where all the Jews meet together: I have said nothing in secret. But why ask me? Ask my hearers what I taught: they know what I said.

N At these words, one of the guards standing by gave Jesus a slap in the face, saying,

S Is that the way to answer the high priest?

N Jesus replied,

✝ If there is something wrong in what I said, point it out; but if there is no offence in it, why do you strike me?

N Then Annas sent him, still bound, to Caiaphas, the high priest.

As Simon Peter stood there warming himself, someone said to him,

S Aren't you another of his disciples?

N He denied it saying,

S I am not.

N One of the high priest's servants, a relation of the man whose ear Peter had cut off, said,

S Didn't I see you in the garden with him?

N Again Peter denied it; and at once a cock crew.

They then led Jesus from the house of Caiaphas to the Praetorium. It was now morning. They did not go into the Praetorium themselves or they would be defiled and unable to eat the passover. So Pilate came outside to them and said,

S What charge do you bring against this man?

N They replied,

C If he were not a criminal, we should not be handing him over to you.

N Pilate said,

S Take him yourselves, and try him by your own Law.

N The Jews answered,

C We are not allowed to put a man to death.

N This was to fulfil the words Jesus had spoken indicating the way he was going to die.

So Pilate went back into the Praetorium and called Jesus to him, and asked,

S Are you the king of the Jews?

N Jesus replied,

† Do you ask this of your own accord, or have others spoken to you about me?

N Pilate answered,

S Am I a Jew? It is your own people and the chief priests who have handed you over to me: what have you done?

N Jesus replied,

† Mine is not a kingdom of this world; if my kingdom were of this world, my men would have fought to prevent me being surrendered to the Jews. But my kingdom is not of this kind.

N Pilate said,

S So you are a king then?

N Jesus answered,

† It is you who say it. Yes, I am a king. I was born for this, I came into the world for this: to bear witness to the truth; and all who are on the side of truth listen to my voice.

N Pilate said,

S Truth? What is that?

N And with that he went out again to the Jews and said,

S I find no case against him. But according to a custom of yours I should release one prisoner at the Passover; would you like me, then, to release the king of the Jews?

N At this they shouted:

C Not this man, but Barabbas.

N Barabbas was a brigand.

Pilate then had Jesus taken away and scourged; and after this, the soldiers twisted some thorns into a crown and put it on his head, and dressed him in a purple robe. They kept coming up to him and saying,

C Hail, king of the Jews!

N and they slapped him in the face.
   Pilate came outside again and said to them,
S Look, I am going to bring him out to you to let you see
   that I find no case.
N Jesus then came out wearing the crown of thorns and
   the purple robe. Pilate said,
S Here is the man.
N When they saw him the chief priests and the guards
   shouted,
C Crucify him! Crucify him!
N Pilate said,
S Take him yourselves and crucify him: I can find no case
   against him.
N The Jews replied,
C We have a Law, and according to the Law he ought to
   die, because he has claimed to be the son of God.
N When Pilate heard them say this his fears increased. Re-
   entering the Praetorium, he said to Jesus,
S Where do you come from?
N But Jesus made no answer. Pilate then said to him,
S Are you refusing to speak to me? Surely you know I have
   power to release you and I have power to crucify you?
N Jesus replied,
† You would have no power over me if it had not been
   given you from above; that is why the one who handed
   me over to you has the greater guilt.
N From that moment Pilate was anxious to set him free,
   but the Jews shouted,
C If you set him free you are no friend of Caesar's; anyone
   who makes himself king is defying Caesar.
N Hearing these words, Pilate had Jesus brought out,
   and seated himself on the chair of judgement at a
   place called the Pavement, in Hebrew Gabbatha. It was
   Passover Preparation Day, about the sixth hour. Pilate
   said to the Jews,
S Here is your king.
N They said,
C Take him away, take him away! Crucify him!

N   Pilate said,

S   Do you want me to crucify your king?

N   The chief priests answered,

C   We have no king except Caesar.

N   So in the end Pilate handed him over to them to be crucified.

They then took charge of Jesus, and carrying his own cross he went out of the city to the place of the skull, or, as it was called in Hebrew, Golgotha, where they crucified him with two others, one on either side with Jesus in the middle. Pilate wrote out a notice and had it fixed to the cross; it ran: "Jesus the Nazarene, King of the Jews." This notice was read by many of the Jews, because the place where Jesus was crucified was not far from the city, and the writing was in Hebrew, Latin and Greek. So the Jewish chief priests said to Pilate,

C   You should not write "King of the Jews", but "This man said: I am King of the Jews."

N   Pilate answered,

S   What I have written, I have written.

N   When the soldiers had finished crucifying Jesus they took his clothing and divided it into four shares, one for each soldier. His undergarment was seamless, woven in one piece from neck to hem; so they said to one another,

C   Instead of tearing it, let's throw dice to decide who is to have it.

N   In this way the words of scripture were fulfilled:

> They shared out my clothing among them.
> They cast lots for my clothes.

This is exactly what the soldiers did.
Near the cross of Jesus stood his mother and his mother's sister, Mary the wife of Clopas, and Mary of Magdala. Seeing his mother and the disciple he loved standing near her, Jesus said to his mother,

✝   Woman, this is your son.

N   Then to the disciple he said,

✝   This is your mother.

N   And from that moment the disciple made a place for her in his home.
After this, Jesus knew that everything had now been completed, and to fulfil the scripture perfectly he said:

✝   I am thirsty.

N   A jar full of vinegar stood there, so putting a sponge soaked in vinegar on a hyssop stick they held it up to his mouth. After Jesus had taken the vinegar he said,

✝   It is accomplished;

N   and bowing his head he gave up the spirit.

(All kneel and pause for a moment.)

N   It was Preparation Day, and to prevent the bodies remaining on the cross during the sabbath – since that sabbath was a day of special solemnity – the Jews asked Pilate to have the legs broken and the bodies taken away. Consequently the soldiers came and broke the legs of the first man who had been crucified with him and then of the other. When they came to Jesus, they found he was already dead, and so instead of breaking his legs one of the soldiers pierced his side with a lance; and immediately there came out blood and water. This is the evidence of one who saw it – trustworthy evidence, and he knows he speaks the truth – and he gives it so that you may believe as well. Because all this happened to fulfil the words of scripture:

Not one bone of his will be broken,

and again, in another place scripture says:

They will look on the one whom they have pierced.

After this, Joseph of Arimathaea, who was a disciple of Jesus – though a secret one because he was afraid of the

Jews – asked Pilate to let him remove the body of Jesus.
Pilate gave permission, so they came and took it away.
Nicodemus came as well – the same one who had first
come to Jesus at night-time – and he brought a mixture
of myrrh and aloes, weighing about a hundred pounds.
They took the body of Jesus and wrapped it with the
spices in linen cloths, following the Jewish burial
custom. At the place where he had been crucified there
was a garden, and in the garden a new tomb in which no
one had yet been buried. Since it was the Jewish Day of
Preparation and the tomb was near at hand, they laid
Jesus there.

The Solemn Intercessions

The deacon, or a lay minister if no deacon is
present, introduces each intercession. After a
period of silent prayer, the priest sings or says the
intercession.

I. For Holy Church

Let us pray, dearly beloved, for the holy Church of God,
that our God and Lord be pleased to give her peace,
to guard her and to unite her throughout the whole world
and grant that, leading our life in tranquillity and quiet,
we may glorify God the Father almighty.

Silent prayer

Almighty ever-living God,
who in Christ revealed your glory to all the nations,
watch over the works of your mercy,
that your Church, spread throughout all the world,
may persevere with steadfast faith in confessing your name.
Through Christ our Lord.
Amen.

II. **For the Pope**

Let us pray also for our most Holy Father Pope N.,
that our God and Lord,
who chose him for the Order of Bishops,
may keep him safe and unharmed for the Lord's holy Church,
to govern the holy People of God.

Silent prayer

Almighty ever-living God,
by whose decree all things are founded,
look with favour on our prayers
and in your kindness protect the Pope chosen for us,
that, under him, the Christian people,
governed by you their maker,
may grow in merit by reason of their faith.
Through Christ our Lord.
Amen.

III. **For all orders and degrees of the faithful**

Let us pray also for our Bishop N.,
for all Bishops, Priests, and Deacons of the Church
and for the whole of the faithful people.

Silent prayer

Almighty ever-living God,
by whose Spirit the whole body of the Church
is sanctified and governed,
hear our humble prayer for your ministers,
that, by the gift of your grace,
all may serve you faithfully.
Through Christ our Lord.
Amen.

IV. For catechumens

Let us pray also for (our) catechumens,
that our God and Lord
may open wide the ears of their inmost hearts
and unlock the gates of his mercy,
that, having received forgiveness of all their sins
through the waters of rebirth,
they, too, may be one with Christ Jesus our Lord.

Silent prayer

Almighty ever-living God,
who make your Church ever fruitful with new offspring,
increase the faith and understanding of (our) catechumens,
that, reborn in the font of Baptism,
they may be added to the number of your adopted children.
Through Christ our Lord.
Amen.

V. For the unity of Christians

Let us pray also for all our brothers and sisters who believe
in Christ,
that our God and Lord may be pleased,
as they live the truth,
to gather them together and keep them in his one Church.

Silent prayer

Almighty ever-living God,
who gather what is scattered
and keep together what you have gathered,
look kindly on the flock of your Son,
that those whom one Baptism has consecrated
may be joined together by integrity of faith
and united in the bond of charity.
Through Christ our Lord.
Amen.

VI. For the Jewish people

Let us pray also for the Jewish people,
to whom the Lord our God spoke first,
that he may grant them to advance in love of his name
and in faithfulness to his covenant.

Silent prayer

Almighty ever-living God,
who bestowed your promises on Abraham and his
    descendants,
graciously hear the prayers of your Church,
that the people you first made your own
may attain the fullness of redemption.
Through Christ our Lord.
Amen.

VII. For those who do not believe in Christ

Let us pray also for those who do not believe in Christ,
that, enlightened by the Holy Spirit,
they, too, may enter on the way of salvation.

Silent prayer

Almighty ever-living God,
grant to those who do not confess Christ
that, by walking before you with a sincere heart,
they may find the truth
and that we ourselves, being constant in mutual love
and striving to understand more fully the mystery of your life,
may be made more perfect witnesses to your love in the world.
Through Christ our Lord.
Amen.

VIII. For those who do not believe in God

Let us pray also for those who do not acknowledge God,
that, following what is right in sincerity of heart,
they may find the way to God himself.

Almighty ever-living God,
who created all people
to seek you always by desiring you
and, by finding you, come to rest,
grant, we pray,
that, despite every harmful obstacle,
all may recognise the signs of your fatherly love
and the witness of the good works
done by those who believe in you,
and so in gladness confess you,
the one true God and Father of our human race.
Through Christ our Lord.
Amen.

IX. **For those in public office**
Let us pray also for those in public office,
that our God and Lord
may direct their minds and hearts according to his will
for the true peace and freedom of all.

Silent prayer

Almighty ever-living God,
in whose hand lies every human heart
and the rights of peoples,
look with favour, we pray,
on those who govern with authority over us,
that throughout the whole world,
the prosperity of peoples,
the assurance of peace,
and freedom of religion
may through your gift be made secure.
Through Christ our Lord.
Amen.

X. For those in tribulation

Let us pray, dearly beloved,
to God the Father almighty,
that he may cleanse the world of all errors,
banish disease, drive out hunger,
unlock prisons, loosen fetters,
granting to travellers safety, to pilgrims return,
health to the sick, and salvation to the dying.

Silent prayer

Almighty ever-living God,
comfort of mourners, strength of all who toil,
may the prayers of those who cry out in any tribulation
come before you,
that all may rejoice,
because in their hour of need
your mercy was at hand.
Through Christ our Lord.
Amen.

Second Part
THE ADORATION OF THE HOLY CROSS

Showing of the Holy Cross

Behold the wood of the Cross,
on which hung the salvation of the world.
Come, let us adore.

Adoration of the Holy Cross

Any of the following or other suitable songs may be sung.

Antiphon

We adore your Cross, O Lord,
we praise and glorify your holy Resurrection,
for behold, because of the wood of a tree
joy has come to the whole world.

33

May God have mercy on us and bless us;
may he let his face shed its light upon us
and have mercy on us.

And the antiphon is repeated:

We adore…

The Reproaches I

1 and 2: My people, what have I done to you?
Or how have I grieved you? Answer me!
1: Because I led you out of the land of Egypt,
   you have prepared a Cross for your Saviour.
1: Hagios o Theos,
2: Holy is God,
1: Hagios Ischyros,
2: Holy and Mighty,
1: Hagios Athanatos, eleison himas.
2: Holy and Immortal One, have mercy on us.

1 and 2: Because I led you out through the desert forty years
and fed you with manna and brought you into a land of plenty,
you have prepared a Cross for your Saviour.
1: Hagios o Theos,
2: Holy is God,
1: Hagios Ischyros,
2: Holy and Mighty,
1: Hagios Athanatos, eleison himas.
2: Holy and Immortal One, have mercy on us.

1 and 2: What more should I have done for you and
have not done?
Indeed, I planted you as my most beautiful chosen vine
and you have turned very bitter for me,
for in my thirst you gave me vinegar to drink
and with a lance you pierced your Saviour's side.
1: Hagios o Theos,
2: Holy is God,
1: Hagios Ischyros,
2: Holy and Mighty,

34

1: Hagios Athanatos, eleison himas.
2: Holy and Immortal One, have mercy on us.

The Reproaches II

Cantors: I scourged Egypt for your sake with its firstborn sons,
and you scourged me and handed me over.

1 and 2: My people, what have I done to you?
Or how have I grieved you? Answer me!

Cantors: I led you out from Egypt as Pharaoh lay sunk in
    the Red Sea,
and you handed me over to the chief priests.

1 and 2: My people...

Cantors: I opened up the sea before you,
and you opened my side with a lance.

1 and 2: My people...

Cantors: I went before you in a pillar of cloud,
and you led me into Pilate's palace.

1 and 2: My people...

Cantors: I fed you with manna in the desert,
and on me you rained blows and lashes.

1 and 2: My people...

Cantors: I gave you saving water from the rock to drink,
and for drink you gave me gall and vinegar.

1 and 2: My people...

Cantors: I struck down for you the kings of the Canaanites,
and you struck my head with a reed.

1 and 2: My people...

Cantors: I put in your hand a royal sceptre,
and you put on my head a crown of thorns.

1 and 2: My people...

Cantors: I exalted you with great power,
and you hung me on the scaffold of the Cross.

1 and 2: My people...

Hymn

All:
**Faithful Cross the Saints rely on,
Noble tree beyond compare!
Never was there such a scion,
Never leaf or flower so rare.
Sweet the timber, sweet the iron,
Sweet the burden that they bear!**

Cantors:
Sing, my tongue, in exultation
Of our banner and device!
Make a solemn proclamation
Of a triumph and its price:
How the Saviour of creation
Conquered by his sacrifice!

All:
**Faithful Cross the Saints rely on,
Noble tree beyond compare!
Never was there such a scion,
Never leaf or flower so rare.**

Cantors:
For, when Adam first offended,
Eating that forbidden fruit,
Not all hopes of glory ended
With the serpent at the root:
Broken nature would be mended
By a second tree and shoot.

All:
Sweet the timber, sweet the iron,
Sweet the burden that they bear!

Cantors:
Thus the tempter was outwitted
By a wisdom deeper still:
Remedy and ailment fitted,
Means to cure and means to kill;
That the world might be acquitted,
Christ would do his Father's will.

All:
Faithful Cross the Saints rely on,
Noble tree beyond compare!
Never was there such a scion,
Never leaf or flower so rare.

Cantors:
So the Father, out of pity
For our self-inflicted doom,
Sent him from the heavenly city
When the holy time had come:
He, the Son and the Almighty,
Took our flesh in Mary's womb.

All:
Sweet the timber, sweet the iron,
Sweet the burden that they bear!

Cantors:
Hear a tiny baby crying,
Founder of the seas and strands;
See his virgin Mother tying
Cloth around his feet and hands;
Find him in a manger lying
Tightly wrapped in swaddling-bands!

All:
Faithful Cross the Saints rely on,
Noble tree beyond compare!
Never was there such a scion,
Never leaf or flower so rare.

Cantors:
So he came, the long-expected,
Not in glory, not to reign;
Only born to be rejected,
Choosing hunger, toil and pain,
Till the scaffold was erected
And the Paschal Lamb was slain.

All:
Sweet the timber, sweet the iron,
Sweet the burden that they bear!

Cantors:
No disgrace was too abhorrent:
Nailed and mocked and parched he died;
Blood and water, double warrant,
Issue from his wounded side,
Washing in a mighty torrent
Earth and stars and oceantide.

All:
Faithful Cross the Saints rely on,
Noble tree beyond compare!
Never was there such a scion,
Never leaf or flower so rare.

Cantors:

Lofty timber, smooth your roughness,
Flex your boughs for blossoming;
Let your fibres lose their toughness,
Gently let your tendrils cling;
Lay aside your native gruffness,
Clasp the body of your King!

All:
Sweet the timber, sweet the iron,
Sweet the burden that they bear!

Cantors:

Noblest tree of all created,
Richly jewelled and embossed:
Post by Lamb's blood consecrated;
Spar that saves the tempest-tossed;
Scaffold-beam which, elevated,
Carries what the world has cost!

All:
Faithful Cross the Saints rely on,
Noble tree beyond compare!
Never was there such a scion,
Never leaf or flower so rare.

Wisdom, power, and adoration
To the blessed Trinity
For redemption and salvation
Through the Paschal Mystery,
Now, in every generation,
And for all eternity. Amen.

Third Part
HOLY COMMUNION

All stand in silence as the Blessed Sacrament
is brought from the place of repose to the altar.

At the Saviour's command
and formed by divine teaching,
we dare to say:

Our Father, who art in heaven,
hallowed be thy name;
thy kingdom come,
thy will be done
on earth as it is in heaven.
Give us this day our daily bread,
and forgive us our trespasses,
as we forgive those who trespass against us;
and lead us not into temptation,
but deliver us from evil.

Deliver us, Lord, we pray, from every evil,
graciously grant peace in our days,
that, by the help of your mercy,
we may be always free from sin
and safe from all distress,
as we await the blessed hope
and the coming of our Saviour, Jesus Christ.

For the kingdom,
the power and the glory are yours
now and for ever.

Behold the Lamb of God,
behold him who takes away the sins of the world.
Blessed are those called to the supper of the Lamb.

Lord, I am not worthy
that you should enter under my roof,
but only say the word
and my soul shall be healed.

Prayer after Communion

Almighty ever-living God,
who have restored us to life
by the blessed Death and Resurrection of your Christ,
preserve in us the work of your mercy,
that, by partaking of this mystery,
we may have a life unceasingly devoted to you.
Through Christ our Lord.

Amen.

Prayer over the People

May abundant blessing, O Lord, we pray,
descend upon your people,
who have honoured the Death of your Son
in the hope of their resurrection:
may pardon come,
comfort be given,
holy faith increase,
and everlasting redemption be made secure.
Through Christ our Lord.

Amen.

After genuflecting to the Cross, all depart in silence.

Easter Vigil

All day today the church has been silent. We have been waiting in prayerful expectation, reflecting on the love of God, confident of the triumph of God's love over pain, suffering and death.

Tonight we celebrate the Resurrection of our Lord at our Easter Vigil. Tonight we share in a special way in the glory of the risen Christ.

The Easter Vigil is in four parts:

Part One is the Lucernarium, or Service of Light – new fire is kindled and blessed. From that fire comes the light for the Easter Candle symbolising Christ who dispels the darkness of the night. The Candle is placed high on the sanctuary and the joyful song of the Easter Proclamation (Exsultet) is sung, as we rejoice in all that this light symbolises for us and for our world in the new life of Christ.

Part Two is the Liturgy of the Word – the story of our salvation is told once more. We relive the story. As we listen to the Old Testament narrative our trust in the promise of redemption and hope for men and women is rekindled.

Part Three is the Liturgy of Baptism – through our baptism we share in the risen life of Christ and are called to share in his work of redeeming the world. Tonight we celebrate with those who are being baptised and we recall our own baptism. We renew our personal baptismal promises and reflect on their significance for us.

Part Four is the Liturgy of the Eucharist – in which we are fully united with Christ and nurtured for our journey until we are one with him in our own resurrection. This is the night of all nights to give thanks and praise to our heavenly Father.

The Easter Vigil in the Holy Night

Part One
THE SOLEMN BEGINNING OF THE VIGIL

The Blessing of Fire and Preparation of the Candle

Dear brethren (brothers and sisters),
on this most sacred night,
in which our Lord Jesus Christ
passed over from death to life,
the Church calls upon her sons and daughters,
scattered throughout the world,
to come together to watch and pray.
If we keep the memorial
of the Lord's paschal solemnity in this way,
listening to his word and celebrating his mysteries,
then we shall have the sure hope
of sharing his triumph over death
and living with him in God.

Let us pray.

O God, who through your Son
bestowed upon the faithful the fire of your glory,
sanctify ✠ this new fire, we pray,
and grant that,
by these paschal celebrations,
we may be so inflamed with heavenly desires,
that with minds made pure
we may attain festivities of unending splendour.
Through Christ our Lord.
Amen.

The paschal candle is brought to the priest to be prepared before it is lit from the Easter fire.

Christ yesterday and today;
the Beginning and the End;
the Alpha;
and the Omega.
All time belongs to him;
and all the ages.
To him be glory and power;
through every age and for ever. Amen.

By his holy
and glorious wounds,
may Christ the Lord
guard us
and protect us. Amen.

May the light of Christ rising in glory
dispel the darkness of our hearts and minds.

Procession

As the paschal candle is processed to the sanctuary, the following is sung three times.

The Light of Christ.
Thanks be to God.

Easter Proclamation (Exsultet)

Exult, let them exult, the hosts of heaven,
exult, let Angel ministers of God exult,
let the trumpet of salvation
sound aloud our mighty King's triumph!
Be glad, let earth be glad, as glory floods her,
ablaze with light from her eternal King,
let all corners of the earth be glad,
knowing an end to gloom and darkness.
Rejoice, let Mother Church also rejoice,

arrayed with the lightning of his glory,
let this holy building shake with joy,
filled with the mighty voices of the peoples.

(Therefore, dearest friends,
standing in the awesome glory of this holy light,
invoke with me, I ask you,
the mercy of God almighty,
that he, who has been pleased to number me,
though unworthy, among the Levites,
may pour into me his light unshadowed,
that I may sing this candle's perfect praises.)

(The Lord be with you.
And with your spirit.)

Lift up your hearts.
We lift them up to the Lord.

Let us give thanks to the Lord our God.
It is right and just.

It is truly right and just,
with ardent love of mind and heart
and with devoted service of our voice,
to acclaim our God invisible, the almighty Father,
and Jesus Christ, our Lord, his Son, his Only Begotten.

Who for our sake paid Adam's debt to the eternal Father,
and, pouring out his own dear Blood,
wiped clean the record of our ancient sinfulness.

These then are the feasts of Passover,
in which is slain the Lamb, the one true Lamb,
whose Blood anoints the doorposts of believers.

This is the night,
when once you led our forebears, Israel's children,
from slavery in Egypt

and made them pass dry-shod through the Red Sea.
This is the night
that with a pillar of fire
banished the darkness of sin.

This is the night
that even now, throughout the world,
sets Christian believers apart from worldly vices
and from the gloom of sin,
leading them to grace
and joining them to his holy ones.

This is the night,
when Christ broke the prison-bars of death
and rose victorious from the underworld.

Our birth would have been no gain,
had we not been redeemed.
O wonder of your humble care for us!
O love, O charity beyond all telling,
to ransom a slave you gave away your Son!

O truly necessary sin of Adam,
destroyed completely by the Death of Christ!

O happy fault
that earned so great, so glorious a Redeemer!

O truly blessed night,
worthy alone to know the time and hour
when Christ rose from the underworld!

This is the night
of which it is written:
The night shall be as bright as day,
dazzling is the night for me,
and full of gladness.

The sanctifying power of this night

dispels wickedness, washes faults away,
restores innocence to the fallen, and joy to mourners,
drives out hatred, fosters concord, and brings down
    the mighty.

On this, your night of grace, O holy Father,
accept this candle, a solemn offering,
the work of bees and of your servants' hands,
an evening sacrifice of praise,
this gift from your most holy Church.

But now we know the praises of this pillar,
which glowing fire ignites for God's honour,
a fire into many flames divided,
yet never dimmed by sharing of its light,
for it is fed by melting wax,
drawn out by mother bees
to build a torch so precious.

O truly blessed night,
when things of heaven are wed to those of earth,
and divine to the human.

Therefore, O Lord,
we pray you that this candle,
hallowed to the honour of your name,
may persevere undimmed,
to overcome the darkness of this night.

Receive it as a pleasing fragrance,
and let it mingle with the lights of heaven.
May this flame be found still burning
by the Morning Star:
the one Morning Star who never sets,
Christ your Son,
who, coming back from death's domain,
has shed his peaceful light on humanity,
and lives and reigns for ever and ever.
Amen.

Part Two
THE LITURGY OF THE WORD

Dear brethren (brothers and sisters),
now that we have begun our solemn Vigil,
let us listen with quiet hearts to the Word of God.
Let us meditate on how God in times past saved his people
and in these, the last days, has sent us his Son as our Redeemer.
Let us pray that our God may complete this paschal work
    of salvation
by the fullness of redemption.

First Reading (Genesis 1:1 – 2:2)
A reading from the book of Genesis

In the beginning God created the heavens and
the earth.

Now the earth was a formless void, there was darkness over
the deep, and God's spirit hovered over the water.

God said, "Let there be light", and there was light.
God saw that light was good, and God divided light from
darkness. God called light "day", and darkness he called
"night". Evening came and morning came: the first day.

God said, "Let there be a vault in the waters to divide
the waters in two." And so it was. God made the vault, and
it divided the waters above the vault from the waters under
the vault. God called the vault "heaven". Evening came and
morning came: the second day.

God said, "Let the waters under heaven come together
into a single mass, and let dry land appear." And so it was.
God called the dry land "earth" and the mass of waters
"seas", and God saw that it was good.

God said, "Let the earth produce vegetation: seed-
bearing plants, and fruit trees bearing fruit with their seed
inside, on the earth." And so it was. The earth produced
vegetation: plants bearing seed in their several kinds,
and trees bearing fruit with their seed inside in their
several kinds. God saw that it was good. Evening came and
morning came: the third day.

God said, "Let there be lights in the vault of heaven to divide day from night, and let them indicate festivals, days and years. Let them be lights in the vault of heaven to shine on the earth." And so it was. God made the two great lights: the greater light to govern the day, the smaller light to govern the night, and the stars. God set them in the vault of heaven to shine on the earth, to govern the day and the night and to divide light from darkness. God saw that it was good. Evening came and morning came: the fourth day.

God said, "Let the waters teem with living creatures, and let birds fly above the earth within the vault of heaven." And so it was. God created great sea-serpents and every kind of living creature with which the waters teem, and every kind of winged creature. God saw that it was good. God blessed them, saying "Be fruitful, multiply, and fill the waters of the seas; and let the birds multiply upon the earth." Evening came and morning came: the fifth day.

God said, "Let the earth produce every kind of living creature: cattle, reptiles, and every kind of wild beast." And so it was. God made every kind of wild beast, every kind of cattle, and every kind of land reptile. God saw that it was good.

God said, "Let us make man in our own image, in the likeness of ourselves, and let them be masters of the fish of the sea, the birds of heaven, the cattle, all the wild beasts and all the reptiles that crawl upon the earth."

> God created man in the image of himself,
> in the image of God he created him,
> male and female he created them.

God blessed them, saying to them, "Be fruitful, multiply, fill the earth and conquer it. Be masters of the fish of the sea, the birds of heaven and all living animals on the earth." God said, "See, I give you all the seed-bearing plants that are upon the whole earth, and all the trees with seed-bearing fruit; this shall be your food. To all wild beasts, all birds of heaven and all living reptiles on the earth I give all the foliage of plants for food." And so it was. God saw all he had made, and indeed it was very good. Evening came and morning came: the sixth day.

Thus heaven and earth were completed with all their array. On the seventh day God completed the work he had been doing. He rested on the seventh day after all the work he had been doing.

The word of the Lord.

Psalm (Psalm 103)

Response: **Send forth your spirit, O Lord,
and renew the face of the earth.**

1 Bless the Lord, my soul!
Lord God, how great you are,
clothed in majesty and glory,
wrapped in light as in a robe! R.

2 You founded the earth on its base,
to stand firm from age to age.
You wrapped it with the ocean like a cloak:
the waters stood higher than the mountains. R.

3 You make springs gush forth in the valleys:
they flow in between the hills.
On their banks dwell the birds of heaven;
from the branches they sing their song. R.

4 From your dwelling you water the hills;
earth drinks its fill of your gift.
You make the grass grow for the cattle
and the plants to serve man's needs. R.

5 How many are your works, O Lord!
In wisdom you have made them all.
The earth is full of your riches.
Bless the Lord, my soul! R.

Alternative Psalm (Psalm 32)

Response: **The Lord fills the earth with his love.**

1   The word of the Lord is faithful
    and all his works to be trusted.
    The Lord loves justice and right
    and fills the earth with his love. R.

2   By his word the heavens were made,
    by the breath of his mouth all the stars.
    He collects the waves of the ocean;
    he stores up the depths of the sea. R.

3   They are happy, whose God is the Lord,
    the people he has chosen as his own.
    From the heavens the Lord looks forth,
    he sees all the children of men. R.

4   Our soul is waiting for the Lord.
    The Lord is our help and our shield.
    May your love be upon us, O Lord,
    as we place all our hope in you. R.

Prayer

Let us pray.

Almighty ever-living God,
who are wonderful in the ordering of all your works,
may those you have redeemed understand
that there exists nothing more marvellous
than the world's creation in the beginning
except that, at the end of the ages,
Christ our Passover has been sacrificed.
Who lives and reigns for ever and ever.
Amen.

or

O God, who wonderfully created human nature
and still more wonderfully redeemed it,
grant us, we pray,
to set our minds against the enticements of sin,
that we may merit to attain eternal joys.
Through Christ our Lord.
Amen.

Second Reading (Genesis 22:1-18)
A reading from the book of Genesis

God put Abraham to the test. "Abraham, Abraham," he
called. "Here I am," he replied. "Take your son," God said,
"your only child Isaac, whom you love, and go to the land
of Moriah. There you shall offer him as a burnt offering,
on a mountain I will point out to you."

Rising early next morning Abraham saddled his ass
and took with him two of his servants and his son Isaac. He
chopped wood for the burnt offering and started on his
journey to the place God had pointed out to him. On the
third day Abraham looked up and saw the place in the
distance. Then Abraham said to his servants, "Stay here
with the donkey. The boy and I will go over there; we will
worship and come back to you."

Abraham took the wood for the burnt offering,
loaded it on Isaac, and carried in his own hands the fire and
the knife. Then the two of them set out together. Isaac
spoke to his father Abraham, "Father," he said. "Yes, my
son," he replied. "Look," he said, "here are the fire and the
wood, but where is the lamb for the burnt offering?"
Abraham answered, "My son, God himself will
provide the lamb for the burnt offering." Then the two of
them went on together.

When they arrived at the place God had pointed out
to him, Abraham built an altar there, and arranged the
wood. Then he bound his son Isaac and put him on the
altar on top of the wood. Abraham stretched out his
hand and seized the knife to kill his son.

But the angel of the Lord called to him from heaven. "Abraham, Abraham," he said. "I am here," he replied. "Do not raise your hand against the boy," the angel said. "Do not harm him, for now I know you fear God. You have not refused me your son, your only son." Then looking up, Abraham saw a ram caught by its horns in a bush. Abraham took the ram and offered it as a burnt-offering in place of his son.

Abraham called this place "The Lord provides", and hence the saying today: On the mountain the Lord provides.

The angel of the Lord called Abraham a second time from heaven. "I swear by my own self – it is the Lord who speaks – because you have done this, because you have not refused me your son, your only son, I will shower blessings on you, I will make your descendants as many as the stars of heaven and the grains of sand on the seashore. Your descendants shall gain possession of the gates of their enemies. All the nations of the earth shall bless themselves by your descendants, as a reward for your obedience."

The word of the Lord.

Psalm (Psalm 15)

Response: **Preserve me, God, I take refuge in you.**

1   O Lord, it is you who are my portion and cup;
        it is you yourself who are my prize.
        I keep the Lord ever in my sight:
        since he is at my right hand, I shall stand firm. R.

2   And so my heart rejoices, my soul is glad;
        even my body shall rest in safety.
        For you will not leave my soul among the dead,
        nor let your beloved know decay. R.

3   You will show me the path of life,
        the fullness of joy in your presence,
        at your right hand happiness for ever. R.

53

Prayer

Let us pray.

O God, supreme Father of the faithful,
who increase the children of your promise
by pouring out the grace of adoption
throughout the whole world
and who through the Paschal Mystery
make your servant Abraham father of nations,
as once you swore,
grant, we pray,
that your peoples may enter worthily
into the grace to which you call them.
Through Christ our Lord.
Amen.

Third Reading (Exodus 14:15 – 15:1)
A reading from the book of Exodus

The Lord said to Moses, "Why do you cry to me so? Tell the
sons of Israel to march on. For yourself, raise your staff
and stretch out your hand over the sea and part it for the
sons of Israel to walk through the sea on dry ground. I for
my part will make the heart of the Egyptians so stubborn
that they will follow them. So shall I win myself glory at
the expense of Pharaoh, of all his army, his chariots, his
horsemen. And when I have won glory for myself at the
expense of Pharaoh and his chariots and his army, the
Egyptians will learn that I am the Lord."

Then the angel of the Lord, who marched at the front
of the army of Israel, changed station and moved to their
rear. The pillar of cloud changed station from the front to
the rear of them, and remained there. It came between the
camp of the Egyptians and the camp of Israel. The cloud
was dark, and the night passed without the armies drawing
any closer the whole night long. Moses stretched out his
hand over the sea. The Lord drove back the sea with a
strong easterly wind all night, and he made dry land of the

sea. The waters parted and the sons of Israel went on dry ground right into the sea, walls of water to right and to left of them. The Egyptians gave chase: after them they went, right into the sea, all Pharaoh's horses, his chariots, and his horsemen. In the morning watch, the Lord looked down on the army of the Egyptians from the pillar of fire and of cloud, and threw the army into confusion. He so clogged their chariot wheels that they could scarcely make headway. "Let us flee from the Israelites," the Egyptians cried, "the Lord is fighting for them against the Egyptians!" "Stretch out your hand over the sea," the Lord said to Moses, "that the waters may flow back on the Egyptians and their chariots and their horsemen." Moses stretched out his hand over the sea and, as day broke, the sea returned to its bed. The fleeing Egyptians marched right into it, and the Lord overthrew the Egyptians in the very middle of the sea. The returning waters overwhelmed the chariots and the horsemen of Pharaoh's whole army, which had followed the Israelites into the sea; not a single one of them was left. But the sons of Israel had marched through the sea on dry ground, walls of water to right and to left of them. That day, the Lord rescued Israel from the Egyptians, and Israel saw the Egyptians lying dead on the shore. Israel witnessed the great act that the Lord had performed against the Egyptians, and the people venerated the Lord; they put their faith in the Lord and in Moses, his servant.

It was then that Moses and the sons of Israel sang this song in honour of the Lord:

Psalm (Exodus 15:1-6. 17-18)

Response: **I will sing to the Lord, glorious his triumph!**

1   I will sing to the Lord, glorious his triumph!
       Horse and rider he has thrown into the sea!
       The Lord is my strength, my song, my salvation.
       This is my God and I extol him,
       my father's God and I give him praise. R.

2 The Lord is a warrior! The Lord is his name.
  The chariots of Pharaoh he hurled into the sea,
  the flower of his army is drowned in the sea.
  The deeps hide them; they sank like a stone. R.

3 Your right hand, Lord, glorious in its power,
  your right hand, Lord, has shattered the enemy.
  In the greatness of your glory you crushed the foe. R.

4 You will lead your people and plant them on
   your mountain,
  the place, O Lord, where you have made your home,
  the sanctuary, Lord, which your hands have made.
  The Lord will reign for ever and ever. R.

Prayer

Let us pray.

O God, whose ancient wonders
remain undimmed in splendour even in our day,
for what you once bestowed on a single people,
freeing them from Pharaoh's persecution
by the power of your right hand
now you bring about as the salvation of the nations
through the waters of rebirth,
grant, we pray, that the whole world
may become children of Abraham
and inherit the dignity of Israel's birthright.
Through Christ our Lord.
Amen.

or

O God, who by the light of the New Testament
have unlocked the meaning
of wonders worked in former times,
so that the Red Sea prefigures the sacred font
and the nation delivered from slavery

foreshadows the Christian people,
grant, we pray, that all nations,
obtaining the privilege of Israel by merit of faith,
may be reborn by partaking of your Spirit.
Through Christ our Lord.
Amen.

Fourth Reading (Isaiah 54:5-14)
A reading from the prophet Isaiah

Thus says the Lord:

Now your creator will be your husband,
his name, the Lord of hosts;
your redeemer will be the Holy One of Israel,
he is called the God of the whole earth.
Yes, like a forsaken wife, distressed in spirit,
the Lord calls you back.
Does a man cast off the wife of his youth?
says your God.

I did forsake you for a brief moment,
but with great love will I take you back.
In excess of anger, for a moment
I hid my face from you.
But with everlasting love I have taken pity on you,
says the Lord, your redeemer.

I am now as I was in the days of Noah
when I swore that Noah's waters
should never flood the world again.
So now I swear concerning my anger with you
and the threats I made against you;
for the mountains may depart,
the hills be shaken,
but my love for you will never leave you
and my covenant of peace with you will never be shaken,
says the Lord who takes pity on you.

Unhappy creature, storm-tossed, disconsolate,
see, I will set your stones on carbuncles
and your foundations on sapphires.
I will make rubies your battlements,
your gates crystal,
and your entire wall precious stones.
Your sons will all be taught by the Lord.
The prosperity of your sons will be great.
You will be founded on integrity;
remote from oppression, you will have nothing to fear;
remote from terror, it will not approach you.

The word of the Lord.

Psalm (Psalm 29)

Response: **I will praise you, Lord, you have rescued me.**

1   I will praise you, Lord, you have rescued me
     and have not let my enemies rejoice over me.
     O Lord, you have raised my soul from the dead,
     restored me to life from those who sink into the grave. R.

2   Sing psalms to the Lord, you who love him,
     give thanks to his holy name.
     His anger lasts but a moment; his favour through life.
     At night there are tears, but joy comes with dawn. R.

3   The Lord listened and had pity.
     The Lord came to my help.
     For me you have changed my mourning into dancing.
     O Lord my God, I will thank you for ever. R.

Prayer

Let us pray.

Almighty ever-living God,
surpass, for the honour of your name,
what you pledged to the Patriarchs by reason of their faith,
and through sacred adoption increase the children of
    your promise,
so that what the Saints of old never doubted would come
    to pass
your Church may now see in great part fulfilled.
Through Christ our Lord.
Amen.

Fifth Reading (Isaiah 55:1-11)

A reading from the prophet Isaiah

Thus says the Lord:

Oh, come to the water all you who are thirsty;
though you have no money, come!
Buy corn without money, and eat,
and, at no cost, wine and milk.
Why spend money on what is not bread,
your wages on what fails to satisfy?
Listen, listen to me, and you will have good things to eat
and rich food to enjoy.
Pay attention, come to me;
listen, and your soul will live.

With you I will make an everlasting covenant
out of the favours promised to David.
See, I have made of you a witness to the peoples,
a leader and a master of the nations.
See, you will summon a nation you never knew,
those unknown will come hurrying to you,
for the sake of the Lord your God,
of the Holy One of Israel who will glorify you.

Seek the Lord while he is still to be found,
call to him while he is still near.
Let the wicked man abandon his way,
the evil man his thoughts.
Let him turn back to the Lord who will take pity on him,
to our God who is rich in forgiving;
for my thoughts are not your thoughts,
my ways not your ways – it is the Lord who speaks.
Yes, the heavens are as high above earth
as my ways are above your ways,
my thoughts above your thoughts.

Yes, as the rain and the snow come down from the heavens
and do not return without watering the earth, making it
yield and giving growth to provide seed for the sower and
bread for the eating, so the word that goes from my mouth
does not return to me empty, without carrying out my will
and succeeding in what it was sent to do.

The word of the Lord.

Psalm (Isaiah 12:2-6)

Response: **With joy you will draw water from the
wells of salvation.**

1 Truly God is my salvation,
I trust, I shall not fear.
For the Lord is my strength, my song,
he became my saviour.
With joy you will draw water
from the wells of salvation. R.

2 Give thanks to the Lord, give praise to his name!
Make his mighty deeds known to the peoples,
declare the greatness of his name. R.

3 Sing a psalm to the Lord
for he has done glorious deeds,
make them known to all the earth!
People of Zion, sing and shout for joy
for great in your midst is the Holy One of Israel. R.

Prayer

Let us pray.

Almighty ever-living God,
sole hope of the world,
who by the preaching of your Prophets
unveiled the mysteries of this present age,
graciously increase the longing of your people,
for only at the prompting of your grace
do the faithful progress in any kind of virtue.
Through Christ our Lord.
Amen.

Sixth Reading (Baruch 3:9-15. 32 – 4:4)

A reading from the prophet Baruch

Listen, Israel, to commands that bring life;
hear, and learn what knowledge means.
Why, Israel, why are you in the country of your enemies,
growing older and older in an alien land,
sharing defilement with the dead,
reckoned with those who go to Sheol?
Because you have forsaken the fountain of wisdom.
Had you walked in the way of God,
you would have lived in peace for ever.
Learn where knowledge is, where strength,
where understanding, and so learn
where length of days is, where life,
where the light of the eyes and where peace.
But who has found out where she lives,
who has entered her treasure house?

But the One who knows all knows her,
he has grasped her with his own intellect,
he has set the earth firm for ever
and filled it with four-footed beasts,
he sends the light – and it goes,
he recalls it – and trembling it obeys;
the stars shine joyfully at their set times:

when he calls them, they answer, "Here we are";
they gladly shine for their creator.
It is he who is our God,
no other can compare with him.
He has grasped the whole way of knowledge,
and confided it to his servant Jacob,
to Israel his well-beloved;
so causing her to appear on earth
and move among men.

This is the book of the commandments of God,
the Law that stands for ever;
those who keep her live,
those who desert her die.
Turn back, Jacob, seize her,
in her radiance make your way to light:
do not yield your glory to another,
your privilege to a people not your own.
Israel, blessed are we:
what pleases God has been revealed to us.
    The word of the Lord.

Psalm (Psalm 18)

Response: **You have the message of eternal life,
O Lord.**

1   The law of the Lord is perfect,
      it revives the soul.
      The rule of the Lord is to be trusted,
      it gives wisdom to the simple. R.

2   The precepts of the Lord are right,
      they gladden the heart.
      The command of the Lord is clear,
      it gives light to the eyes. R.

3   The fear of the Lord is holy,
        abiding for ever.
        The decrees of the Lord are truth
        and all of them just. R.

4   They are more to be desired than gold,
        than the purest of gold
        and sweeter are they than honey,
        than honey from the comb. R.

Prayer

Let us pray.

O God, who constantly increase your Church
by your call to the nations,
graciously grant
to those you wash clean in the waters of Baptism
the assurance of your unfailing protection.
Through Christ our Lord.
Amen.

Seventh Reading (Ezekiel 36:16-28)
A reading from the prophet Ezekiel

The word of the Lord was addressed to me as follows: "Son of man, the members of the House of Israel used to live in their own land, but they defiled it by their conduct and actions. I then discharged my fury at them because of the blood they shed in their land and the idols with which they defiled it. I scattered them among the nations and dispersed them in foreign countries. I sentenced them as their conduct and actions deserved. And now they have profaned my holy name among the nations where they have gone, so that people say of them, 'These are the people of the Lord; they have been exiled from his land.' But I have been concerned about my holy name, which the House of Israel has profaned among the nations where they have gone. And so, say to the House of Israel, 'The Lord says this: I am not doing this for your sake, House of Israel, but for the sake of my holy name, which you have profaned among the nations where you have gone. I mean to display the holiness of my great name, which has been profaned among the nations, which you have profaned among them. And the nations will learn that I am the Lord – it is the Lord who speaks – when I display my holiness for your sake before their eyes. Then I am going to take you from among the nations and gather you together from all the foreign countries, and bring you home to your own land. I shall pour clean water over you and you will be cleansed; I shall cleanse you of all your defilement and all your idols. I shall give you a new heart, and put a new spirit in you; I shall remove the heart of stone from your bodies and give you a heart of flesh instead. I shall put my spirit in you, and make you keep my laws and sincerely respect my observances. You will live in the land which I gave your ancestors. You shall be my people and I will be your God.'"

The word of the Lord.

Psalm (Psalms 41 and 42)

Response: **Like the deer that yearns for running streams, so my soul is yearning for you, my God.**

1 My soul is thirsting for God,
   the God of my life;
   when can I enter and see
   the face of God? R.

2 These things will I remember
   as I pour out my soul:
   how I would lead the rejoicing crowd
   into the house of God,
   amid cries of gladness and thanksgiving,
   the throng wild with joy. R.

64

3   O send forth your light and your truth;
        let these be my guide.
        Let them bring me to your holy mountain
        to the place where you dwell. R.

4   And I will come to the altar of God,
        the God of my joy.
        My redeemer, I will thank you on the harp,
        O God, my God. R.

If there are candidates to be baptised, one of the
following Psalms is used instead:

Isaiah 12 (after fifth reading, page 60) or Psalm 50
as follows:

Response: **A pure heart create for me, O God.**

1   A pure heart create for me, O God,
        put a steadfast spirit within me.
        Do not cast me away from your presence,
        nor deprive me of your holy spirit. R.

2   Give me again the joy of your help;
        with a spirit of fervour sustain me,
        that I may teach transgressors your ways
        and sinners may return to you. R.

3   For in sacrifice you take no delight,
        burnt offering from me you would refuse,
        my sacrifice, a contrite spirit.
        A humbled, contrite heart you will not spurn. R.

Prayer

Let us pray.

O God of unchanging power and eternal light,
look with favour on the wondrous mystery of the
     whole Church
and serenely accomplish the work of human salvation,
which you planned from all eternity;
may the whole world know and see
that what was cast down is raised up,
what had become old is made new,
and all things are restored to integrity through Christ,
just as by him they came into being.
Who lives and reigns for ever and ever.
Amen.

or

O God, who by the pages of both Testaments
instruct and prepare us to celebrate the Paschal Mystery,
grant that we may comprehend your mercy,
so that the gifts we receive from you this night
may confirm our hope of the gifts to come.
Through Christ our Lord.
Amen.

The Gloria is sung or said, during which the church
bells may be rung.

Collect

O God, who make this most sacred night radiant
with the glory of the Lord's Resurrection,
stir up in your Church a spirit of adoption,
so that, renewed in body and mind,
we may render you undivided service.
Through our Lord Jesus Christ, your Son,
who lives and reigns with you in the unity of the Holy Spirit,
one God, for ever and ever.
Amen.

New Testament Reading (Romans 6:3-11)

A reading from the letter of St Paul to the Romans

When we were baptised in Christ Jesus we were baptised in his death; in other words, when we were baptised we went into the tomb with him and joined him in death, so that as Christ was raised from the dead by the Father's glory, we too might live a new life.

If in union with Christ we have imitated his death, we shall also imitate him in his resurrection. We must realise that our former selves have been crucified with him to destroy this sinful body and to free us from the slavery of sin. When a man dies, of course, he has finished with sin.

But we believe that having died with Christ we shall return to life with him: Christ, as we know, having been raised from the dead will never die again. Death has no power over him any more. When he died, he died, once for all, to sin, so his life now is life with God; and in that way, you too must consider yourselves to be dead to sin but alive for God in Christ Jesus.

The word of the Lord.

Psalm (Psalm 117)

Response: **Alleluia, alleluia, alleluia!**

1   Give thanks to the Lord for he is good,
       for his love has no end.
       Let the sons of Israel say:
       "His love has no end." R.

2   The Lord's right hand has triumphed;
       his right hand raised me up.
       I shall not die, I shall live
       and recount his deeds. R.

3   The stone which the builders rejected
       has become the corner stone.
       This is the work of the Lord,
       a marvel in our eyes. R.

The Gospel for Year A, B or C is read according to the cycle for the year.

Year A
Gospel (Matthew 28:1-10)
A reading from the holy Gospel according to Matthew

After the sabbath, and towards dawn on the first day of the week, Mary of Magdala and the other Mary went to visit the sepulchre. And all at once there was a violent earthquake, for the angel of the Lord, descending from heaven, came and rolled away the stone and sat on it. His face was like lightning, his robe white as snow. The guards were so shaken, so frightened of him, that they were like dead men. But the angel spoke; and he said to the women, "There is no need for you to be afraid. I know you are looking for Jesus, who was crucified. He is not here, for he has risen, as he said he would. Come and see the place where he lay, then go quickly and tell his disciples, 'He has risen from the dead and now he is going before you to Galilee; it is there you will see him.' Now I have told you." Filled with awe and great joy the women came quickly away from the tomb and ran to tell the disciples.

And there, coming to meet them, was Jesus. "Greetings," he said. And the women came up to him and, falling down before him, clasped his feet. Then Jesus said to them, "Do not be afraid; go and tell my brothers that they must leave for Galilee; they will see me there."

The Gospel of the Lord.

Year B
Gospel (Mark 16:1-7)
A reading from the holy Gospel according to Mark

When the sabbath was over, Mary of Magdala, Mary the mother of James, and Salome, brought spices with which to go and anoint him. And very early in the morning on the first day of the week they went to the tomb, just as the sun was rising.

They had been saying to one another, "Who will roll away the stone for us from the entrance to the tomb?" But when they looked they could see that the stone – which was very big – had already been rolled back. On entering the tomb they saw a young man in a white robe seated on the right-hand side, and they were struck with amazement. But he said to them, "There is no need for alarm. You are looking for Jesus of Nazareth, who was crucified: he has risen, he is not here. See, here is the place where they laid him. But you must go and tell his disciples and Peter, 'He is going before you to Galilee; it is there you will see him, just as he told you.'"

The Gospel of the Lord.

Year C
Gospel (Luke 24:1-12)
A reading from the holy Gospel according to Luke

On the first day of the week, at the first sign of dawn, the women went to the tomb with the spices they had prepared. They found that the stone had been rolled away from the tomb, but on entering discovered that the body of the Lord Jesus was not there. As they stood there not knowing what to think, two men in brilliant clothes suddenly appeared at their side. Terrified, the women lowered their eyes. But the two men said to them, "Why look among the dead for someone who is alive? He is not here; he has risen. Remember what he told you when he was still in Galilee: that the Son of Man had to be handed over into the power of sinful men and be crucified, and rise again on the third day?" And they remembered his words.

When the women returned from the tomb they told all this to the Eleven and to all the others. The women were Mary of Magdala, Joanna, and Mary the mother of James. The other women with them also told the apostles, but this story of theirs seemed pure nonsense, and they did not believe them.

Peter, however, went running to the tomb. He bent down and saw the binding cloths, but nothing else; he then went back home, amazed at what had happened.

The Gospel of the Lord.

Part Three
BAPTISMAL LITURGY

If there are candidates to be baptised:

Dearly beloved,
with one heart and one soul, let us by our prayers
come to the aid of these our brothers and sisters in their
    blessed hope,
so that, as they approach the font of rebirth,
the almighty Father may bestow on them
all his merciful help.

If the font is to be blessed, but no one is to be baptised:

Dearly beloved,
let us humbly invoke upon this font
the grace of God the almighty Father,
that those who from it are born anew
may be numbered among the children of adoption in Christ.

Litany of the Saints

All stand.

Lord, have mercy.	**Lord, have mercy.**
Christ, have mercy.	**Christ, have mercy.**
Lord, have mercy.	**Lord, have mercy.**
Holy Mary, Mother of God,	**pray for us.**
Saint Michael,	**pray for us.**
Holy Angels of God,	**pray for us.**
Saint John the Baptist,	**pray for us.**
Saint Joseph,	**pray for us.**
Saint Peter and Saint Paul,	**pray for us.**
Saint Andrew,	**pray for us.**
Saint John,	**pray for us.**
Saint Mary Magdalene,	**pray for us.**
Saint Stephen,	**pray for us.**
Saint Ignatius of Antioch,	**pray for us.**
Saint Lawrence,	**pray for us.**

Saint Perpetua and Saint Felicity,	**pray for us.**
Saint Agnes,	**pray for us.**
Saint Gregory,	**pray for us.**
Saint Augustine,	**pray for us.**
Saint Athanasius,	**pray for us.**
Saint Basil,	**pray for us.**
Saint Martin,	**pray for us.**
Saint Benedict,	**pray for us.**
Saint Francis and Saint Dominic,	**pray for us.**
Saint Francis Xavier,	**pray for us.**
Saint John Vianney,	**pray for us.**
Saint Catherine of Siena,	**pray for us.**
Saint Teresa of Jesus,	**pray for us.**
All holy men and women, Saints of God,	**pray for us.**
Lord, be merciful,	**Lord, deliver us, we pray.**
From all evil,	**Lord, deliver us, we pray.**
From every sin,	**Lord, deliver us, we pray.**
From everlasting death,	**Lord, deliver us, we pray.**
By your Incarnation,	**Lord, deliver us, we pray.**
By your Death and Resurrection,	**Lord, deliver us, we pray.**
By the outpouring of the Holy Spirit,	**Lord, deliver us, we pray.**
Be merciful to us sinners,	**Lord, we ask you, hear our prayer.**

If there are candidates to be baptised:

Bring these chosen ones to new birth through the grace
   of Baptism,
Lord, we ask you, hear our prayer.

If there is no one to be baptised:

Make this font holy by your grace for the new birth of
   your children,
Lord, we ask you, hear our prayer.

Jesus, Son of the living God,
Lord, we ask you, hear our prayer.

Christ, hear us.
Christ, hear us.

Christ, graciously hear us.
Christ, graciously hear us.

If there are candidates to be baptised:

Almighty ever-living God,
be present by the mysteries of your great love
and send forth the spirit of adoption
to create the new peoples
brought to birth for you in the font of Baptism,
so that what is to be carried out by our humble service
may be brought to fulfilment by your mighty power.
Through Christ our Lord.
Amen.

Blessing of Baptismal Water

O God, who by invisible power
accomplish a wondrous effect
through sacramental signs
and who in many ways have prepared water, your creation,
to show forth the grace of Baptism;
O God, whose Spirit
in the first moments of the world's creation

hovered over the waters,
so that the very substance of water
would even then take to itself the power to sanctify;

O God, who by the outpouring of the flood
foreshadowed regeneration,
so that from the mystery of one and the same element of water
would come an end to vice and a beginning of virtue;

O God, who caused the children of Abraham
to pass dry-shod through the Red Sea,
so that the chosen people,
set free from slavery to Pharaoh,
would prefigure the people of the baptised;

O God, whose Son,
baptised by John in the waters of the Jordan,
was anointed with the Holy Spirit,
and, as he hung upon the Cross,
gave forth water from his side along with blood,
and after his Resurrection, commanded his disciples:
"Go forth, teach all nations, baptising them
in the name of the Father and of the Son and of the Holy Spirit",
look now, we pray, upon the face of your Church
and graciously unseal for her the fountain of Baptism.

May this water receive by the Holy Spirit
the grace of your Only Begotten Son,
so that human nature, created in your image,
and washed clean through the Sacrament of Baptism
from all the squalor of the life of old,
may be found worthy to rise to the life of newborn children
through water and the Holy Spirit.

May the power of the Holy Spirit,
O Lord, we pray,
come down through your Son
into the fullness of this font,
so that all who have been buried with Christ

by Baptism into death
may rise again to life with him.
Who lives and reigns with you in the unity of the Holy Spirit,
one God, for ever and ever.
Amen.

**Springs of water, bless the Lord;
praise and exalt him above all for ever.**

After the baptismal water has been blessed, those
who are to be baptised profess their faith. Then they
are baptised and, if appropriate, confirmed.

If no one is to be baptised and the font is not to be
blessed:

Blessing of Water

Dear brothers and sisters,
let us humbly beseech the Lord our God
to bless this water he has created,
which will be sprinkled upon us
as a memorial of our Baptism.
May he graciously renew us,
that we may remain faithful to the Spirit
whom we have received.

Lord our God,
in your mercy be present to your people
who keep vigil on this most sacred night,
and, for us who recall the wondrous work of our creation
and the still greater work of our redemption,
graciously bless this water.
For you created water to make the fields fruitful
and to refresh and cleanse our bodies.
You also made water the instrument of your mercy:
for through water you freed your people from slavery
and quenched their thirst in the desert;
through water the Prophets proclaimed the new covenant
you were to enter upon with the human race;
and last of all,

through water, which Christ made holy in the Jordan,
you have renewed our corrupted nature
in the bath of regeneration.
Therefore, may this water be for us
a memorial of the Baptism we have received,
and grant that we may share
in the gladness of our brothers and sisters,
who at Easter have received their Baptism.
Through Christ our Lord.
Amen.

Renewal of Baptismal Promises

Dear brethren (brothers and sisters),
   through the Paschal Mystery
we have been buried with Christ in Baptism,
so that we may walk with him in newness of life.
And so, now that our Lenten observance is concluded,
let us renew the promises of Holy Baptism,
by which we once renounced Satan and his works
and promised to serve God in the holy Catholic Church.
And so I ask you:

Do you renounce Satan?
I do.

And all his works?
I do.

And all his empty show?
I do.

or

Do you renounce sin,
so as to live in the freedom of the children of God?
I do.

Do you renounce the lure of evil,
so that sin may have no mastery over you?
I do.

Do you renounce Satan,
the author and prince of sin?
I do.

Do you believe in God,
the Father almighty,
Creator of heaven and earth?
I do.

Do you believe in Jesus Christ, his only Son, our Lord,
who was born of the Virgin Mary,
suffered death and was buried,
rose again from the dead
and is seated at the right hand of the Father?
I do.

Do you believe in the Holy Spirit,
the holy Catholic Church,
the communion of saints,
the forgiveness of sins,
the resurrection of the body,
and life everlasting?
I do.

And may almighty God, the Father of our Lord Jesus Christ,
who has given us new birth by water and the Holy Spirit
and bestowed on us forgiveness of our sins,
keep us by his grace,
in Christ Jesus our Lord,
for eternal life.
Amen.

As the priest sprinkles the people with the baptismal
water, the following antiphon or another suitable
song may be sung.

I saw water flowing from the Temple,
from its right-hand side, alleluia;
and all to whom this water came were saved
and shall say: Alleluia, alleluia.

Part Four

THE LITURGY OF THE EUCHARIST

Prayer over the Offerings

Accept, we ask, O Lord,
the prayers of your people
with the sacrificial offerings,
that what has begun in the paschal mysteries
may, by the working of your power,
bring us to the healing of eternity.
Through Christ our Lord.
Amen.

The Eucharistic Prayer

The Lord be with you.
And with your spirit.

Lift up your hearts.
We lift them up to the Lord.

Let us give thanks to the Lord our God.
It is right and just.

It is truly right and just, our duty and our salvation,
at all times to acclaim you, O Lord,
but on this night above all
to laud you yet more gloriously,
when Christ our Passover has been sacrificed.

For he is the true Lamb
who has taken away the sins of the world;
by dying he has destroyed our death,
and by rising, restored our life.

Therefore, overcome with paschal joy,
every land, every people exults in your praise
and even the heavenly Powers, with the angelic hosts,
sing together the unending hymn of your glory,
as they acclaim:

Holy, Holy, Holy Lord God of hosts.
Heaven and earth are full of your glory.
Hosanna in the highest.
Blessed is he who comes in the name of the Lord.
Hosanna in the highest.

Communion Antiphon

Christ our Passover has been sacrificed;
therefore let as keep the feast
with the unleavened bread of purity and truth,
  alleluia.

Prayer after Communion

Pour out on us, O Lord, the Spirit of your love,
and in your kindness make those you have nourished
by this paschal Sacrament
one in mind and heart.
Through Christ our Lord.
Amen.

Solemn Blessing

May almighty God bless you
through today's Easter Solemnity
and, in his compassion,
defend you from every assault of sin.
Amen.

And may he, who restores you to eternal life
in the Resurrection of his Only Begotten,
endow you with the prize of immortality.
Amen.

Now that the days of the Lord's Passion have drawn to a close,
may you who celebrate the gladness of the Paschal Feast
come with Christ's help, and exulting in spirit,
to those feasts that are celebrated in eternal joy.
Amen.

And may the blessing of almighty God,
the Father, and the Son, ✠ and the Holy Spirit,
come down on you and remain with you for ever.
Amen.

Dismissal

Go forth, the Mass is ended, alleluia, alleluia.

or

Go in peace, alleluia, alleluia.
Thanks be to God, alleluia, alleluia.

Hymns

1

O bread of heaven, beneath this veil
thou dost my very God conceal;
my Jesus, dearest treasure, hail;
I love thee and adoring kneel;
each loving soul by thee is fed
with thine own self in form of bread.

O food of life, thou who dost give
the pledge of immortality;
I live; no, 'tis not I that live;
God gives me life, God lives in me:
he feeds my soul, he guides my ways,
and every grief with joy repays.

O bond of love, that dost unite
the servant to his living Lord;
could I dare live, and not requite
such love – then death were meet reward:
I cannot live unless to prove
some love for such unmeasured love.

Beloved Lord in heaven above,
there, Jesus, thou awaitest me;
to gaze on thee with changeless love,
yes, thus I hope, thus shall it be:
for how can he deny me heaven
who here on earth himself hath given?

St Alphonsus Liguori (1696–1787),
tr. E. Vaughan

2

Godhead here in hiding,
whom I do adore,
masked by these bare shadows,
shape and nothing more,
see, Lord, at thy service
low lies here a heart
lost, all lost in wonder
at the God thou art.

Seeing, touching, tasting
are in thee deceived;
how says trusty hearing?
That shall be believed;
what God's Son hath told me,
take for truth I do;
truth himself speaks truly,
or there's nothing true.

On the cross thy Godhead
made no sign to men;
here thy very manhood
steals from human ken;
both are my confession,
both are my belief;
and I pray the prayer
of the dying thief.

I am not like Thomas,
wounds I cannot see,
but can plainly call thee
Lord and God as he;
this faith each day deeper
be my holding of,
daily make me harder
hope and dearer love.

O thou our reminder
of Christ crucified,
living Bread, the life of
us for whom he died,
lend this life to me then;
feed and feast my mind,
there be thou the sweetness
man was meant to find.

Jesu, whom I look at
shrouded here below,
I beseech thee send me
what I long for so,
some day to gaze on thee
face to face in light
and be blest for ever
with thy glory's sight.

*Ascribed to St Thomas Aquinas
(1227–74),
tr. Gerard Manley Hopkins*

3

My song is love unknown,
my Saviour's love to me,
love to the loveless shown,
that they might lovely be.
O who am I, that for my sake,
my Lord should take frail flesh and die?

He came from his blest throne,
salvation to bestow;
but men made strange, and none
the longed-for Christ would know,
but O my friend, my friend indeed,
who at my need his life did spend!

Sometimes they strew his way,
and his sweet praises sing;
resounding all the day
hosannas to their King;
then "Crucify!" is all their breath,
and for his death they thirst and cry.

Why, what hath my Lord done?
What makes this rage and spite?
He made the lame to run,
he gave the blind their sight.
Sweet injuries! Yet they at these
themselves displease, and 'gainst him rise.

They rise, and needs will have
my dear Lord made away;
a murderer they save,
the Prince of Life they slay.
Yet cheerful he to suffering goes,
that he his foes from thence might free.

In life, no house, no home
my Lord on earth might have:
in death no friendly tomb
but what a stranger gave.
What may I say? Heaven was his home;
but mine the tomb wherein he lay.

Here might I stay and sing,
no story so divine,
never was love, dear King,
never was grief like thine.
This is my Friend, in whose sweet praise
I all my days could gladly spend.

Samuel Crossman (c.1624–83)

4

When I survey the wondrous cross
on which the Prince of Glory died,
my richest gain I count but loss,
and pour contempt on all my pride.

Forbid it, Lord, that I should boast,
save in the death of Christ, my God:
all the vain things that charm me most,
I sacrifice them to his blood.

See from his head, his hands, his feet,
sorrow and love flow mingled down:
did e'er such love and sorrow meet,
or thorns compose so rich a crown?

His dying crimson like a robe,
spreads o'er his body on the Tree;
then I am dead to all the globe,
and all the globe is dead to me.

Were the whole realm of nature mine,
that were an offering far too small;
love so amazing, so divine,
demands my soul, my life, my all.

Isaac Watts (1674–1748)

5

Glory be to Jesus,
who in bitter pains
poured for me the life-blood,
from his sacred veins.

Grace and life eternal
in that blood I find:
blest be his compassion,
infinitely kind.

Blest through endless ages
be the precious stream,
which from endless torment
doth the world redeem.

There the fainting spirit
drinks of life her fill;
there as in a fountain
laves herself at will.

Abel's blood for vengeance
pleaded to the skies,
but the blood of Jesus
for our pardon cries.

Oft as it is sprinkled
on our guilty hearts,
Satan in confusion
terror-struck departs.

Oft as earth exulting
wafts its praise on high,
hell with horror trembles;
heaven is filled with joy.

Lift ye, then, your voices;
swell the mighty flood;
louder still and louder,
praise the precious blood.

18th century, tr. Edward Caswall

6

Christ the Lord is risen today!
Christians, haste your vows to pay,
offer ye your praises meet
at the paschal victim's feet;
for the sheep the Lamb hath bled,
sinless in the sinner's stead.
Christ the Lord is ris'n on high;
now he lives, no more to die.

Christ, the victim undefiled,
man to God hath reconciled
when in strange and awful strife
met together death and life;
Christians, on this happy day
haste with joy your vows to pay.
Christ the Lord is ris'n on high;
now he lives, no more to die.

Say, O wond'ring Mary, say,
what thou sawest on thy way.
"I beheld, where Christ had lain,
empty tomb and angels twain,
I beheld the glory bright
of the rising Lord of light;
Christ my hope is ris'n again;
now he lives, and lives to reign."

Christ, who once for sinners bled,
now the first-born from the dead,
throned in endless might and power,
lives and reigns for evermore.
Hail, eternal hope on high!
Hail, thou King of victory!
Hail, thou Prince of life adored!
Help and save us, gracious Lord.

Wipo, 11th century,
tr. Jane Elizabeth Leeson

7

At the Lamb's high feast we sing
praise to our victorious king,
who hath washed us in the tide
flowing from his pierced side.
Praise we him whose love divine
gives the guests his blood for wine,
gives his body for the feast,
love the victim, love the priest.

Where the paschal blood is poured,
Death's dark angel sheathes his sword;
Israel's hosts triumphant go
through the wave that drowns the foe.
Christ the Lamb, whose blood was shed,
paschal victim, paschal bread;
with sincerity and love
eat we manna from above.

Mighty victim from the sky,
powers of hell beneath thee lie;
death is conquered in the fight;
thou hast brought us life and light,
now thy banner thou dost wave;
vanquished Satan and the grave;
angels join his praise to tell –
see o'erthrown the prince of hell.

Paschal triumph, paschal joy,
only sin can this destroy;
from the death of sin set free
souls re-born, dear Lord, in thee.
Hymns of glory, songs of praise,
Father, unto thee we raise.
Risen Lord, all praise to thee,
ever with the Spirit be.

7th century, tr. Robert Campbell